Joint Task Force – Guantanamo Bay, Cuba: Open or Close?

The president said he was issuing the order to close the facility in order to "restore the standards of due process and the core constitutional values that have made this country great even in the midst of war, even in dealing with terrorism." January 22, 2009.

—President Obama

On 22 January 2009, President Obama issued an executive order calling for the Guantanamo Bay, Cuba (GTMO), detention facility to be closed within one year. The President had been sworn in just a few days before. He immediately launched an ambitious agenda, ranging from health care reform to passing a massive financial package to stimulate a struggling economy. Still, the decision to close GTMO was a top priority; so the executive order to close it was one of President Obama's first acts in office. It has been four years since President Obama signed that executive order directing the closure of detention operations at Guantanamo Bay. Subsequently, despite domestically political and international scrutiny, detention operations at Guantanamo Bay, Cuba have evolved into the premier detention facility in the world. This Strategy Research Project addresses the evolution of detention operations at GTMO. It weighs the advantages and disadvantages of keeping this most strategic and high profile facility open.

Why GTMO?

United States Naval Station Guantanamo Bay is the oldest U.S. base overseas and the only one in a communist country with which the U.S. does not maintain diplomatic relations. Located on the southeast corner of Cuba, the base is about 400 miles from Miami, Florida. In February 1903, the United States leased 45 square miles of land and water at Guantanamo Bay to use as a coaling station. As technology advanced, it evolved into a refueling station. In December 1903, the treaty was finalized, and signed in Havana. Another treaty reaffirmed the lease in 1934; it granted Cuba and her trading partners free access through the bay, payment of $2,000 in gold per year ($4,085 today), and required that both the United States and Cuba must mutually consent to terminate the lease.[1]

In 1961 diplomatic relations with Cuba were severed by President Dwight Eisenhower. At that time, many Cubans sought refuge on the base. U.S. Marines and Cuban militiamen then began patrolling opposite sides of the base's 17.4 mile fence line. Today, U.S. Marines and Cuba's "Frontier Brigade" still man fence-line posts 24 hours a day.   In October 1962, family members of military personnel and many base employees were evacuated to the United States when President John F. Kennedy announced the presence of Soviet missiles in Cuba.[2] This signal led the start of the Cuban Missile Crisis, which resulted in a U.S. naval quarantine of the island until the Soviet Union removed the missiles. The evacuees were allowed to return to the base by Christmas 1962. Another crisis arose just 14 months later on 6 February 1964, when Castro cut off water and supplies to the base in retaliation for several incidents in which Cuban fisherman were fined by the U.S. government for fishing in Florida waters. Since then, Guantanamo Bay has been self-sufficient, and the base desalination plant produces 3.4 kilowatt-hours of electricity daily. [3]

The base is divided into two separate areas by the 2 ½ mile-wide Guantanamo Bay. The airfield is located on the leeward side, and the main base is on the windward side. Ferry services provide transportation across the bay. The primary mission of this facility is to serve as a strategic logistics base for the Navy's Atlantic Fleet (fuel and supplies), to support counter-drug operations in the Caribbean, and to serve as the primary location for migrant surge operations in the Caribbean. [4]

The installation's remote location enables the Department of Defense (DoD) to monitor aircraft flights and control maritime access points, thereby providing an additional layer of security for the detention operations. This unique location gave U.S. leaders an area to establish a detention facility in a secure and isolated location, deny the detainees any opportunity to rejoin the fight. In addition, this Cuban site allowed U.S. officials to avoid bringing individuals suspected of terrorism onto domestic soil.

The Legal Basis for Detaining Al Qaida and Taliban Combatants

The United States and its coalition partners are engaged in a war against Al-Qaida, the Taliban, and their affiliates and supporters. There is no question that under the law of war the United States has the authority to detain persons who have engaged in unlawful belligerence for the duration of hostilities, without charges or trial. As with all wars, no one knows when this one will end. Nevertheless, the country may detain combatants until the end of the war.[5]

Detention of enemy combatants in wartime is not an act of punishment. Rather, it is a matter of security and military necessity; it has long been recognized as legitimate under international law. The U.S. Supreme Court, in Hamdi v. Rumsfeld, 542 U.S. 507 (2004), specifically recognized the authority of the President to detain persons who fought for the Taliban and Al Qaida against the United States.[6] Detention of enemy combatants prevents them from returning to the battlefield and engaging in further armed attacks against innocent civilians and U.S. and Coalition forces. Furthermore, detention serves as a deterrent against future attacks by denying the enemy the fighters needed to sustain the war. Releasing enemy combatants before the end of hostilities and allowing them to rejoin the fight could prolong the conflict and further endanger U.S. and Coalition forces and innocent civilians.[7]

There is no requirement under the law of war that a detaining power charge enemy combatants with crimes or gives them lawyers or access to the courts in order to challenge their detention. To the extent that enemy combatants have committed offenses under the law of war, a detaining power may choose to try them. The law of war, which includes the Geneva Conventions, recognizes that military commissions may be used to try persons who engage in belligerent acts in contravention of the law of war. The United States and many other nations have used military commissions throughout history; military commissions have an established and legitimate role in the law of war.[8]

Designed to handle crimes committed in times of war or rebellion, military commissions were used early in this nation's history. General George Washington convened a precursor to a military commission—a board of inquiry—in 1780 to try a British major accused of conspiring with Benedict Arnold during the Revolutionary War. The board recommended to Washington that Major John Andre be executed: He was promptly hanged. The first documented use of military commissions came during the Mexican-American War in 1847, when the U.S. Army occupied large areas of Mexico that lacked a working court system. Since then, military commissions have been used to prosecute thousands in the U.S. and abroad during the Civil War, Reconstruction, the Spanish-American War, and World War II. Defendants have included a former Ohio congressman accused of sympathizing with the Confederacy during the Civil War (ordered confined for the rest of the war), eight accused conspirators in President Lincoln's assassination (four sentenced to hang, four given prison sentences), and eight

4

Germans accused of arriving in the U.S. by submarine to carry out sabotage attacks (six were electrocuted).[9]

The Third Geneva Convention of 1949 accords Prisoner of War (POW) status generally only to enemy forces that follow certain rules: They are commanded by a person responsible for subordinates. They have donned a fixed, distinctive uniform recognizable at a distance. They carry arms openly. They conduct operations in accordance with the laws and customs of war. President George W. Bush determined that although the Geneva Convention applies to Taliban detainees, such detainees are not entitled to POW status. As explained by the White House press secretary on 7 February 2002:

> Under Article 4 of the Geneva Convention. Taliban detainees are not entitled to POW status The Taliban have not effectively distinguished themselves from the civilian population of Afghanistan. Moreover, they have not conducted their operations in accordance with the laws and customs of war.[10]

Regarding Al Qaeda, the statement continues:

> Al Qaeda is an international terrorist group and cannot be considered a state party to the Geneva Convention. Its members, therefore, are not covered by the Geneva Convention, and are not entitled to POW status under the treaty.[11]

Even if detainees were entitled to POW status, they would not have the right to lawyers, access to the courts to challenge their detention, or the opportunity to be released prior to the end of hostilities. Nothing in the Third Geneva Convention provides POWs such rights, and POWs in past wars have generally not been given these rights.[12]

History of Joint Task Force (JTF)-GTMO

Following the 9/11 attacks, a U.S. led Coalition launched military operations in Afghanistan, and quickly captured many members of al Qaida and the Taliban. U.S. officials then decided to transfer a number of detainees to Camp X-Ray, Guantanamo Bay, Cuba. The original facilities were open for 92 days (in 2002). They were preexisting migrant-detention facilities comprised of chain-link enclosures on concrete slabs. The base was originally intended to serve as a temporary holding facility for Al Qaida, Taliban, and other detainees that came under U.S. control during the War on Terrorism.[13]

The U.S. Southern Command (SOUTHCOM) was in charge of the operation. Joint Task Force 160 (JTF-160) was activated to head the detainee operations in January 2002. It included active duty members of the Army, Air Force, Marines, Navy, and Coast Guard. Reserve component personnel were also deployed on the mission. Military police personnel made up the bulk of JTF-160.[14]

JTF-160's primary mission was to take care of captured enemy combatants from the War on Terrorism. It was established in support of detainee operation activities as the holding facility for Al Qaida, Taliban, and other terrorist personnel who came under U.S. control. The unit also provided support to Joint Task Force 170 (JTF-170), which was stood up by SOUTHCOM on 16 February 2002, to coordinate the U.S. military and government agency interrogation efforts in support of Operation Enduring Freedom (OEF). JTF-170 conducted DoD interrogation operations and ensured coordination among government agencies involved in the interrogation of the suspected terrorists. The JTF-170 was established in support of detainee operations; it serves as DoD's focal point for interrogation operations.[15]

As mentioned above, the first detainees arrived at Camp X-Ray on 11 January 2002. As of 1 February 2002, detainee in-processing and questioning at Camp X-Ray had been limited to inquiries about detainees' names, place of birth, time of birth, names of parents and siblings, and education. More in-depth interrogations began shortly thereafter. Camp X-Ray's detention facilities consisted of eight-by-eight units surrounded by wire mesh. Detainees slept on 4 to 5 thick mattresses with sheets and blankets. The mattresses were on the floor, as is Afghan custom. Each unit had a concrete floor with a combination wood/metal overhead cover. The units were separated by chain-link fence, and razor wire and watchtowers surrounded the compound. Guards inside the compound carried no weapons to ensure the safety of both the guards and the detainees. [16]

A change of command on 4 November 2002 merged JTF-160 and JTF-170 to form Joint Task Force Guantanamo (JTF GTMO). JTF GTMO continued the detainee and interrogation operations at Camp Delta.[17] The JTF has three major missions:

> Conduct the safe, humane, legal, and transparent care and custody of detainees, including those convicted by military commission and those ordered released by a court. Conduct intelligence collection, analysis, and dissemination for the protection of detainees and personnel working in JTF Guantanamo facilities and in support of the War on Terror. Provide support to the Office of Military Commissions, to law enforcement, and to war crimes investigations.

Current Conditions at JTF-GTMO

For legal, policy, operational, and medical reasons, JTF-GTMO is required to maintain several camps: Detainees with court-ordered releases must be separated from the general population. Detainees who have been convicted must be separated from non-convicted detainees. High Value Detainees (HVDs) must be separated from the general population for reasons of national security. In-patient medical and psychiatric wards must be maintained for those detainees requiring such medical services. Detainees who have cooperated with intelligence and law enforcement officials must be separated from the general population for their own safety. Camp leaders must be separated from the general population for operational purposes. Finally, within general populations, different levels of detention (communal v. non-communal) must be maintained to encourage compliance with camp rules. All facilities have been greatly improved since detainees first arrived at Camp X-Ray in January 2002.[18]

The majority of GTMO detainees have been transferred elsewhere. The JTF currently holds 166 of the 779 who have been brought to GTMO. During the past several years, there have been on-going efforts to enhance detainee operations. The JTF has consolidated camps from nine to five, to reduce manpower and costs. About 85% of detainees reside in Camps Five and Six, state-of-the-art facilities that were replicated from facilities back in the states.[19] GTMO is widely perceived as a prison. However, understanding the difference between detainees and prisoners is key to understanding JTF GTMO. A prisoner has been convicted of a crime and sentenced to prison where as a detainee is an individual who is held in custody. As mentioned earlier, individuals are being detained at JTF GTMO to keep them out of the fight: They are not there to be punished. [20] In the past, the mention of GTMO might bring to mind dark images of detainees on their knees in orange jumpsuits near open-air chain-link fences. GTMO today consists of state-of-the-art facilities in which detainees get to choose where they live based on their behavior. GTMO currently consists of the following camps:

Camp 5

Completed in 2004 at a cost of $17 million with a capacity of 100. Currently fewer than 15 detainees are housed at Camp 5, the maximum-security camp that houses non-compliant detainees. The camp provides individual climate-controlled cells with beds, sinks, and toilets. Detainees are offered the opportunity to shower daily; they are permitted two to four hours of outside recreation time. As the least compliant detainees, these individuals have the most limited privileges; they are granted television/radio access on a weekly basis. The current manning required for Camp 5 is approximately 80 guards.[21]

Camp 6

Completed in 2006 at a cost of $37 million with a capacity of 176. This medium-security communal camp is minimally guarded. Detainees are assigned individual cells with a bed, sink, and toilet. Detainees are allowed out of their cells for 20 hours per day. The camp is divided into blocks: Each block contains 20 cells with a climate-controlled inside recreation area and an outside recreation area. Showers and satellite televisions and radios are located within the inside recreation area. Each pair of blocks shares a large central recreation area, including a soccer field. Camp 6 detainees are allowed 20 hours in central recreation, which is equipped with deep sinks and fitness equipment. Currently, nearly 200 guards secure Camp 6.[22]

Camp 7

High Value Detainee camp, over which JTF-GTMO assumed control in 2006. Operations and conditions at Camp 7 are coordinated through SOUTHCOM with the Special Detainee Follow-up Group (OSD and Joint Staff). Camp 7 has a guard force and staff of around 125.[23]

Camp Echo

Completed in 2003 with a capacity to house eight detainees, who are considered to be in protective custody due to their cooperation with intelligence and law enforcement officials. Echo West provides private cells with a bed, toilet, sink, and shower, with adjoining private sitting areas. Echo East has two private buildings for special protective custody. Camp Echo also contains 10 combination cells for legal visits (not to house detainees). Camp Echo requires a guard force of approximately 40 personnel.[24]

Camp Iguana

Camp new mission in 2008 was to house detainees who have received court-ordered releases. Camp Iguana has the capacity to hold 22 detainees who live in a complete open, minimum-security environment. The detainees at Camp Iguana have 24-hour access to a recreation area, sleeping berths, and a laundry facility, and they are provided weekly canteen runs to purchase civilian clothes, additional foods, and comfort items not afforded to the other detainees. The guard force required for Camp Iguana is 25.[25]

Medical

Medical care provided for detainees at Guantánamo Bay is of the same quality as that which U.S. service members receive. The lives of several detainees have been saved by the excellent medical treatment provided by U.S. military personnel. Detainees are treated in a dedicated medical facility with state-of-the-art equipment and an expert medical staff of more than 100 personnel. The medical facility is equipped with 20 in-patient beds, a physical therapy area, a pharmacy, radiology department, a central sterilization area, and a single bed for operating. More serious medical conditions can be treated at the naval base hospital operating room and intensive care unit. Specialists are available to provide care for any medical needs that exceed the capabilities of the naval base hospital. In addition to the detainee hospital, there is a separate facility for dedicated mental health care. Most routine medical care is administered by Navy corpsmen who visit each cell block every two days and whenever a detainee requests care. Detainees at GTMO have received immunizations, most of which would not have been available in their home countries. Some detainees have been provided life-changing care, such as prosthetic limbs or surgical removal of cancerous tumors. Psychological care also is available for detainees who may need it.[26]

Intelligence

A civilian director employed by the Defense Intelligence Agency, aided by an O-6 deputy director, leads the Joint Intelligence Group (JIG). The JIG assigns personnel into functional branches, one of which is interrogation. JIG is staffed by analysts, linguists, and information managers. Interrogators work in the Interrogation Control Element (ICE), led by an ICE Chief and Deputy ICE Chief, and assisted by subordinate Section Chiefs and Assistant Section Chiefs.[27]

JTF-Guantánamo schedules interrogations daily, between the hours of 0800 and 1700. Currently all interrogations are voluntary; approximately one-third of the sessions are at detainees' request. These are conducted in strict compliance with Army Field Manual 2-22.3, Human Intelligence Collector Operations (September 2006). Given the length of time that most detainees have spent at Guantánamo, the primary focus of interrogations is to gather security and force protection information related to the operations of the detention camps. The current intelligence mission relies primarily on

11

direct approaches and small incentive items to encourage detainees to volunteer information.[28]

The JTF has been one of the most investigated military operations in U.S. history: the Church Report, (March 2005), Schmidt-Furlow Report, (June 2005), and the Walsh Report, (April 2009). Investigation after investigation has shown that allegations of abuse are just that–allegations. There have been no substantiated cases of "torture" at Guantanamo. Additionally, contrary to popular opinion, water-boarding has never taken place at Guantanamo Bay. [29]

Military Commissions

The Guantanamo military commissions are military tribunals created by the Military Commissions Act of 2006. They are responsible for prosecuting detainees held in the Guantanamo Bay detainment camps. A military tribunal or commission is a court that asserts jurisdiction over persons who are combatants of an enemy force, who are held in military custody, and who are accused of a violation of the laws of war. In contrast, courts-martial generally exercise jurisdiction over only members of their own military. A military tribunal or commission may still use the rules and procedures of a court-martial, although that is not generally the case.[30]

Military tribunals also, generally speaking, do not assert jurisdiction over people who are acknowledged as non-combatants who are alleged to have broken civil or criminal laws. However, military tribunals are sometimes used to try individuals not affiliated with a particular state's military, but who are nonetheless accused of being combatants and acting in violation of the laws of war.[31]

JTF Guantanamo is tasked with supporting military commissions. This task is carried out primarily by managing the facilities; by maintaining the security of the facilities, the detainees, and others involved; and by assisting in the escorting and hosting of media and NGOs. The trials are conducted under the authority of the Office of Military Commissions.[32] The JTF facilitated construction of the Expeditionary Legal Complex. The portion of the complex, known as "Camp Justice" houses many of the military personnel who operate the facility. The complex includes a second new courtroom specifically designed for handling the cases of High Value Detainees, such as the alleged 9-11 co-conspirators. The facility is specifically designed to handle highly classified information.[33]

Each accused detainee receives a copy of the charges in his native language: Outside influence on witnesses and trial participants is prohibited. The accused may challenge members of the commission, and an accused may represent himself or have assistance of counsel. The accused is presumed innocent until guilt is established beyond a reasonable doubt: He is entitled to assistance to secure evidence on his behalf: He is not required to incriminate himself at trial, and his silence is not held against him: He may not be tried a second time for the same offense. Finally, he is entitled to the assistance of counsel through four stages of post-trial appellate review ending at the United States Supreme Court.[34]

Argument for Keeping GTMO Open

Many observers throughout the world believe that Guantanamo Bay is succeeding in its intended purpose. It is keeping captured terrorist suspects from harming anyone, and it is deterring others from committing acts of terrorism. Of course, its critics claim it is a torturous and inhumane prison. There is no question that controversy will continue to surround this detention facility. Since its opening, many on both sides of the issue have debated the value and morality of detention operations at

13

Guantanamo Bay. On 22 January 2009, after only two days in office, President Obama upheld his campaign promise and ordered Guantanamo Bay closed. But Congress has opposed the President's efforts to close the detention facility. Accordingly, President Obama should consider arguments for keeping the facility open.

First, it is important to remember that there are 166 detainees still residing at Guantanamo Bay. If the base is closed, the U.S. will still have to house these individuals somewhere. Former Vice-President Dick Cheney claimed, "If we didn't have that facility at Guantanamo to undertake this activity, we'd have to have it someplace else because they're a vital source of intelligence information. They've given us useful information that has been used in pursuing our aims and objectives in the war on terror."[35]

Another reason to keep Guantanamo Bay open is to make effective use of resources already invested in the current facility. The United States has already heavily invested in infrastructure to ensure Guantanamo Bay meets a high standard for detainee operations. For instance, the government spent approximately $60 million to build the high-security detention facilities.[36] In addition, Guantanamo Bay added a new "expeditionary legal complex" for the military commission trials at a price of $10 to $12 million.[37] Annually, the government spends an estimated $125 million in Guantanamo's operating costs.[38]

If Guantanamo's detention facilities are abandoned it will probably cost this much or more to establish comparable new facilities in the United States to accommodate the remaining detainees, to say nothing about the cost of transporting them securely to new facilities? Why spend this amount of money again, rather than keep the current facilities in operation? Closing Guantanamo clearly does not pass the common sense test. The image of the U.S. will not change overnight with the closing of Guantanamo Bay.

Guantanamo has always been a symbol, rather than the substance, of complaints against the U.S. "war on terror." But it is really the military character of the U.S. response to 9/11 that foreign and domestic critics find unacceptable. Closing the detention facilities will create numerous headaches beyond the security issues raised by domestic housing of dangerous detainees who might escape or serve as a magnet for terrorist attacks in U.S. based facilities. One possible problem is that the Guantanamo detainees may recruit more terrorists from among the federal inmate population and continue Al Qaeda operations from the inside.

A longer term problem is that once Guantanamo is closed, the option of holding captured enemy combatants at any other overseas site will be undermined. Over time, more and more such individuals, including the ones convicted by military commissions, would have to be brought to the U.S. Aggregating the world's worst jihadists on U.S. soil, from which they can never be repatriated, is not a smart way to fight a war. Meanwhile, the legality of incarcerating captured terrorists in U.S. domestic prisons is far from clear. Today, the Guantanamo detainees are held under well-established laws of war that permit belligerents to confine captured enemies until hostilities are over. This detention, without the due process accorded criminal defendants, has always been legally justified because it emphatically is not penal in nature. Rather, it is a simple expedient necessary to keep captives from returning to the fight. It was on this basis that the Supreme Court approved the detention of war-on-terror captives, without trial, in

Hamdi v. Rumsfeld (2004). The Guantanamo detainees are "unlawful" enemy combatants and not "prisoners of war" under the Geneva Conventions. Yet they are still combatants, not convicts.

By contrast, the individuals held in the federal prison system, and especially those in the maximum security facilities suggested for the Guantanamo detainees, are convicted criminals. It is very doubtful that under the customary laws and customs of war, the Hamdi decision, or Common Article 3 of the Geneva Conventions (which the Supreme Court also has applied to the war on terror), the Guantanamo detainees can be treated like convicted criminals and consigned without trial to the genuinely fearsome world of a super-max prison. Segregating the detainees from the overall prison population--to maintain the "non-penal" character of their confinement as well as to frustrate any recruiting activities or continuing Al Qaeda operations--is also legally dubious. Unless a new Guantanamo is to be constructed, this segregation will have to take place in existing isolation wards used to discipline (and sometimes protect) federal inmates. This could mean solitary confinement, perhaps for 23 hours a day, without regard to a detainee's conduct or disciplinary status. The chances are poor that courts would consider this to be the "humane" treatment required by the Geneva conventions. The Obama administration can be certain these conditions will be challenged in the courts, and it is difficult to see how, in light of current judicial attitudes, the detainees would be denied the entire panoply of constitutional rights claimed by ordinary inmates-- including lawsuits challenging their conditions of confinement. If courts conclude that these conditions are unconstitutional, or that they cannot be held indefinitely as enemy combatants, judges could mandate the release of these jihadists into the U.S.

The detainee recidivism rate also plays a big part in the argument to keep the Guantanamo detention facility open. In a summary report dated 5 March 2012, the office of the Director of National Intelligence said that 27.9% of the 599 former detainees released from Guantanamo were either confirmed or suspected of later engaging in militant activity. The figures represent a 2.9% rise over the 25% aggregate recidivism rate reported by the intelligence czar's office in December 2010. Overall, the statistics showed that, of the 599 detainees who were released as of 29 December 2011, 95 were confirmed to have re-engaged in militant activity or to have been in contact with militants. This comprises 15.9% of the total released. Another 72 militants were "suspected of re-engaging" in militant activity after they were freed from Guantanamo. This constitutes an additional 12% of all released detainees.[39] In addition, a large percentage of the remaining 166 detainees at GTMO are Yemeni, which presents a huge issue for transfers because the conditions in Yemen are viewed as too unsettled to assume the detention of militant detainees.

As a member of the Senate Armed Services Committee, Senator Kelly Ayotte (Republican/New Hampshire) has worked to keep the Guantanamo Bay terrorist detention facility open, to keep terrorist detainees out of the United States, and to limit the transfer of detainees from GTMO to foreign countries. On 16 June 2012, Senator Ayotte successfully inserted in the Senate version of the Fiscal Year 2012 Defense Authorization Bill a provision she authored that permanently prohibits funding for the construction or modification of facilities in the United States to house terrorist detainees.[40] The measure was approved by the full committee. In May, Senator Ayotte introduced the Detaining Terrorists to Secure America Act (S. 944), bipartisan legislation that would keep open the Guantanamo Bay facility for the detention and interrogation of current and future terrorists.[41]

Benjamin Wittes, a senior fellow in governance studies at the Brookings Institution, argues that GTMO's facilities will be needed for at least another decade. America needs principles to justify ongoing use of GTMO–principles that might form the basis for a national policy. He outlines three suggestions toward that end. First, the President must face the fact that the efforts to close GTMO have failed. It is clear that Congress has a strong preference to keep GTMO open. What's more, much of the President's political base has realized that closure does not mean much if detainees are moved rather than freed. Second, detainees at GTMO should be granted due process, habeas corpus, and access to lawyers. Third, non-criminal detention is a fluid business that requires flexibility. The ability to free detainees must be unencumbered for any detention policy to work well. Together, these three principles could form the basis for a flexible detention policy for the upcoming decade.[42]

Argument for Closing GTMO

Many critics argue that the Guantanamo Bay detention facility has done irreparable harm to the nation's international standing and moral authority in the eyes of the world. In the process, it has also damaged the country's leadership in human rights causes and heightened anti-American sentiments, especially among Islamic countries. Once thought of as the unequivocal leader of freedom and democracy, the United States now suffers from a tarnished image within the international community and here at home. Amnesty International sees GTMO as a "symbol of injustice and abuse."[43] In May 2006, the Attorney General for England and Wales Lord Goldsmith said the camp's existence was "unacceptable" and tarnished the U.S. traditions of liberty and justice.

18

"The historic tradition of the United States as a beacon of freedom, liberty and of justice deserves the removal of this symbol," he said. [44]Some fear that GTMO creates new threats and alienates our friends and allies. A senior Administration official stated that "Closing the detention center at Guantanamo is essential to protecting our national security and helping our troops by removing a deadly recruiting tool from the hands of al Qaeda."[45]

Many believe that the U.S. criminal justice system has a better track record of prosecuting terrorists than do military commissions. In fact, the civilian courts have been handling international terrorism cases for two decades. Since the 9/11 attacks, civilian courts have prosecuted and convicted more than 400 people with ties to international terrorist organizations. The military commissions have convicted only six in that same period.[46]

Another strong argument for closing GTMO is the legal black hole into which detainee operations have been swallowed. The Bush administration began this detention operation without a thorough understanding of how to treat detainees under the Geneva Conventions and with little regard for legal due process. Although these issues were eventually resolved, there remained a legal vacuum for the detainees.

Conclusion

Passage of a 2013 National Defense Act, which once again prevents the use of DoD funds to transfer detainees from Guantanamo Bay, Cuba, to the United States or elsewhere, effectively makes it impossible for President Obama to fulfill his long-deferred promise to close this highly scrutinized facility. He threatened to veto the bill. But with the looming fiscal cliff, the GTMO closure fell in the black hole of political discord and became an issue not worth fighting for at this time. Guantánamo has largely faded from public attention. There is little reason to expect it to emerge as an issue in the near future beyond the usual finger-pointing. President Obama may blame Congress for manipulating him into keeping the prisoners at Guantánamo rather than moving them somewhere else. In the final analysis, Guantanamo Bay should remain open and continue to house its current population of 166 detainees.

Meanwhile, the detention center just entered its 12th year of operations on 11 January. Guantánamo is arguably the most expensive prison camp on earth, with its staff of 1,850 U.S. troops and civilians managing a compound that contains 166 captives. Of those 166 prisoners, just six are facing Pentagon tribunals that may start a year from now after pretrial hearings and discovery. In the meantime, JTF-Guantánamo will continue to require extensive resources. Enhancement of humane treatment, as the operation in Guantánamo continues to mature and as the detainee population spends more time under U.S. control, will require strengthening of internal controls and continued dedication of both funds and personnel. Several actions must continue in order to maintain high standards of humane treatment. The most important activity in this regard is continued support for camp improvement projects that enable detainees to socialize.

Finally, determination of detainee status greatly affects detainee behavior and, the overall welfare of the camp population. These determinations affect the long-term ability to comply with Common Article 3 of the Geneva Conventions. Ultimately, the detention facility at GTMO provides an imperfect solution to a highly complex problem. Over 82% of all GTMO detainees have already been released; wherever possible, the U.S. government should expedite this process and repatriate those who are no longer believed to pose a substantial threat. At the same time, the accused should appear before some form of court to receive due process. In the end, though, considering the many interests at stake and the absence of good alternatives, this analysis conclude that the GTMO detention facility must remain open for the foreseeable future. As our nation continues to detain these individuals, the administration should seriously consider permitting family visits.

Endnotes

[1] CNIC//Naval Station Guantanamo Bay – History, http://www.cnic.navy.mil/guantanamo/About/History/index.htm (accessed 12 January 2013).

[2] Ibid.

[3] Ibid.

[4] Ibid.

[5] Fact Sheet --The Legal Basis for Detaining Al Qaida and Taliban Combatants, http://www.google.com/search?sourceid=navclient&ie=UTF-8&rlz=1T4TSNO_enUS490US490&q=The+legal+Basis+for+Detaining+Al+Qaida+and+Taliban+Combatants (accessed 20 January 2013).

[6] Ibid.

[7] Ibid.

[8] Ibid.

[9] Randy James, " A Brief History of Military Commissions," Time Magazine, May 18, 2009, http://www.time.com/time/nation/article/0,8599,1899131,00.html (accessed 25 February 2013).

[10] Fact Sheet --The Legal Basis for Detaining Al Qaida and Taliban Combatants, http://www.google.com/search?sourceid=navclient&ie=UTF-8&rlz=1T4TSNO_enUS490US490&q=The+legal+Basis+for+Detaining+Al+Qaida+and+Taliban+Combatants (accessed 20 January 2013).

[11] Ibid.

[12] Ibid.

[13] Fact Sheet–JTF History, 1 Apr 2010, http://www.jtfgtmo.southcom.mil (accessed 20 December 2012).

[14] Ibid.

[15] Ibid.

[16] Ibid.

[17] Ibid.

[18] Fact Sheet–JTF Current Conditions, 1 May 2012 http://www.jtfgtmo.southcom.mil (accessed 20 December 2012).

[19] Ibid.

[20] Ibid.

[21] Ibid.

[22] Ibid.

[23] Ibid.

[24] Ibid.

[25] Ibid.

[26] Fact Sheet-JTF Medical, 1 April 2012, http://www.jtfgtmo.southcom.com.mil (accessed 22 December 2012).

[27] Fact Sheet-JTF Intelligence, 1 April 2012, http://www.jtfgtmo.southcom (accessed 22 December 2012).

[28] Ibid.

[29] Ibid.

[30] Military Commissions, http://www.defenselink.mil/news/commissions.html (accessed 20 December 2012).

[31] Ibid.

[32] Ibid.

[33] Ibid.

[34] Ibid.

[35] MSNBC.com, "Ex-Gitmo Detainee Reportedly Gets al Qaida Role," http://www.msnbc.msn.com/id/28800516 (accessed 20 January 2013).

[36] Bowker and Kaye, "Guantanamo by the Numbers," International Herald Tribune, 13 November 2007, http://www.iht.com/articles/2007/11/13/opinion/edbowker.php (accessed 10 January 2013).

[37] Ibid.

[38] Ibid.

[39] The Director of National Intelligence submits a summary of the Reengagement of Detainees Formerly Held at Guantanamo Bay, Cuba ,Fiscal Year 2012 Intelligence Authorization Act, Section 307,dated March 1, 2012 http://www.dni.gov/index.php/newsroom/reports-and-publications/93-reports-publications-2012/487-summary-of-the-reengagement-of-detainees-formerly-held-at-guantanamo-bay,-cuba

[40] National Defense Authorization Act for Fiscal Year 2012, Section 1026, page 269 Prohibition on Use of Funds to Construct or Modify Facilities in the United States to House Detainee Transferred from United States Naval Station, Guantanamo Bay, Cuba.

[41] Senator Ayotte, S.944 Congressional Record; May 11, 2011(senate), Bill to maintain Detention Facility at Guantanamo Bay, Cuba http://www.fas.org/irp/congress/2011_cr/s944.html (accessed 25 February 2013).

[42] Benjamin Wittes, "How the Next 10 Years of Guantanamo Should Look," Brookings, 11 January 2012, http://www.brookings.edu/research/opinions/2012/01/11-guantanamo-wittes (Date accessed 25 February 2013)

[43] Amnesty International, "Detention and Imprisonment," http://www.amnesty.org/en/detention (accessed 7 March 2012)

[44] BBC News, Uk told US Won't Shut Guantanamo, 11May 2006, http://news.bbc.co.uk/2/hi/uk_news/Politics/4760365.stm(accessed 7 March 2013)

[45] ABC News homepage http://abcnews.go.com/Politics/obama-white-house-announces-transfer-guantanamo-detainees-illinois/story?id=9342554&page=2,(accessed 7 March 2013)

[46] Washington Post, Why Guantanamo isn't the right place to try terror suspects, 29 July 2011, http://articles.washingtonpost.com/2011-07-29/opinions/35267615_1_civilian-courts-guantanamo-bay-international-terrorism-cases,(accessed 25 February 2012)